What Matters First

PALMETTO
PUBLISHING

Charleston, SC
www.PalmettoPublishing.com

What Matters First
Copyright © 2022 by Lloyd Kropp

First Edition

Paperback ISBN: 979-8-8229-0189-6

What Matters First

AND OTHER SELECTED POEMS

Lloyd Kropp

Contents

There is no truth or beauty

if the heart has not loved the impossible.

This gift is given to Carolyn and my sons
And in memory of Connie and Willis

MEDITATIONS

What Matters First

The things that matter first are tenuous.
The shapes of clouds in October
When the air is full of odor and expectation.
Maple leaves fall. Their points turn inward.
They balance, barely touching, on concrete driveways.
Like the hands of an aging pianist.
They are brown and veined, but with traces of green.
They turn in the wind, gathering in small vortices
As they rustle, restless in the slow change of season.

The things that matter first are tenuous.
Downtown at midnight, the man across the street
In a blue raincoat stands alone in the rain
Under a café awning. He waits for someone.

Here in the garden, the interrogation of an owl,
The flutter of unknown creatures at nightfall,
The slow rhythmical rise and fall of cicadas
Tuning their dry wings. I have known
The abrupt end of beautiful things dissected and explained
In bright light. This is why I lose myself in shadows,
Contrasts and harmonies. Wind runs like silk through my fingers
Here in the night garden.

I know I have appointments to keep.
I hear the sirens, and the horns of trucks
On the hillside a mile beyond the wood.
Tomorrow I will wake into a labyrinth of reasons
And divide the day into morning, afternoon and evening.

But as I stand here now in the present tense
I am reluctant to leave the moment.
The things that matter first are tenuous.
They are the only time we have
Since time is always now.

We are too quick to ask what the moon means by shining,
Too determined by the tasks before us
And by the road that seems to go somewhere
To notice small things that pass by so quickly:
Dust that turns to gold in sunlight from an open window,
A bloom of dandelions, the small hands of children,
A blind violinist playing against voices in the subway.
These are the source of all our virtue and goodness.
Curiosity precedes science. Sanctity rests in small things
Even as knowledge lives in the shadow of wonder.

If there is an ending somewhere in space,
Perhaps there is an answer to all our questions
And a meaning to all our striving.
But in the blessed meanwhile we know
That what matters first is tenuous:
> The leaves of October have voices.
> The man across the street looks up into the rain and whistles.
> The dark garden is alive with small things.

Poetry

Poetry is a form of silence.
It is like waiting for the night,
Or hoping that things will turn out well.
It is what happens when you wish to believe in God,
But instead you hear the sound of waves crashing silver on the beach,
And you see sheets of water slipping back into the deep,
Drawing grains of sand and broken shells that teeter
    and roll in the current.
It is watching cliff swallows wheeling in the air over some high place
And knowing, far below, that you too can fly,
And that you live in the spaces between their quick, fluttering heartbeats.

Poetry is a form of stillness.
It is the place you come to when you go nowhere,
And it is what you do when you get there.
It is loving when there is no one to love,
When you are alone with yourself,
And you throw yourself hopelessly against everything
That is impossible and nameless.
Poetry is the gift of nothing. It is what you could not pay for,
The thing you longed to give to someone you never knew.
And so you dreamed the gift into being,
More beautifully and more terribly than it ever could have been.
And as you gave this gift to someone, to no one,
The giving made you whole.

The Artist of the Miniature

With his fingertips he holds knives so fine, so narrow,
They lose their edge if flourished too quickly through the heavy air.
He carves motes of dust into unicorns, into mountains filled with
vague, rising forests,
Using specks of light and dark plucked from under his eyelids
To shape the trees, the shadows, the beasts moving in the half-
realized underbrush.
His subjects are things of the moment frozen in some narrow time:
Daphne melting into a laurel tree. A skimmer racing just above the
ocean's swell.

A change of light at the window moves a tiny space of air
And a day's work is undone, blown away. No matter.
His vision is clear and he begins again.
He must make his strokes just so, and between heartbeats,
Or the faint tremor in his fingers will fault the carving.
All is silence and even temperature, or fragile things dissolve to nothing.

After a day's work, a few strands of dust have coalesced into an
amber nude
With dark nipples, an upraised chin, a hand with fingers reaching
into space.
Her eyes wide open, she seems expectant, on tiptoe, spellbound.
She anticipates her step into emptiness. She lasts eighteen seconds,
Then dissolves to nothing. Less than a smudge.

The exquisite agony and triumph of his discipline,

Is not the days of work to define, to redefine

So that stroke and stillness are versions of the same.

Or to go blind with infinite recession, to cease breathing for a hour

And hold still the air in the room by an act of will.

Not this, but rather the courage to see her beauty in eighteen
    seconds

And to bear the moment of her vanishing.

To make permanent what barely, briefly was.

To be content with the shape of air

left behind when something vanishes

Pteranadons

Strange to think they live inside us, a shadow in our genetic memory.
Observe that boneblack spikes point backward on their skulls,
And see the river-wide batwings, the claws,
The yellow leering eyes of the nightmare,
Trapped, you thought, in slow sediments buried deep.
You will not find them in your western bird book.
You see them only in the elemental shadows of another forest,
Dark in the slant of the afternoon.
A vanished mystery among the elms and maples,
They perch and gape amid the fronds of ancient cycads.
You cannot forget the clusters of grinning yellow beaks,
The black primordial wings, unfoldable,
That point like dark moons into the sky.
They make no sound, but their Mesozoic silence
Is fiercer than the hawking of simple birds.

Last week I saw one fly over Boston.
No one looked up. But at four o'clock on Washington Street
Insurance salesmen suffered brief attacks of vertigo,
Bank officials swallowed pills, gulped water from paper cups,
And secretaries in glass cages, dressed in tailored business suits,
Were suddenly silent in the passing shadow of enormous wings.

Sanctuary

There is Sanctuary in the high windows
And in the wind below that blows through leaves and branches.
Twelve stories down, the boulevards shimmer with light
and the crowded city holds its breath to bring forth a garden,
A park full of sinuous walkways and green silence.
There is Sanctuary in the late afternoon when the plunging sun
Sharpens the dark outlines of buildings sketched against
    the western glow.

I step back from the window and feel Sanctuary in small places.
The corner of a room where a book lies open on the floor,
And a bronze lamp turns motes of dust to silver.

In another room, there is Sanctuary in the upturned faces of children,
In their tiny hands that reach out to us,
And in their small bedtime voices that touch the uncertain darkness.
Later on in sleep, which is the smallest place there is,
There is Sanctuary in dreams shaped from oblivion,
In star journeys and in the dark matter that lies between,
Dark matter whose mystery we rise into and embrace.

I know that for ten thousand years there has been Sanctuary
In circles of fire, and there are men outside the circle who are burned
For what they think, screaming and dancing in the flames until they fall.
The forests are also burning, and in cold, distant places
The ice of the world is melting.
Cities and towns are eaten away by ravenous creatures
Who cannot think or feel beyond their appetites,
And the hapless poor are washed into the sea,
    or flee from the gunfire of patriots full of holy thoughts.

But we cannot take arms against all the evil news
Unless we find a room to rest at night,
A room like this one, high above the city.
We must learn and remember the small useless things.

To find Sanctuary we must imagine that our bodies
Dissolve into nothing, and we become music.
Our melody is a butterfly, a red wagon left in an alleyway,
A secret meadow which is the woman of the world.
She is spellbound as her slow harmony turns from season to season,
Turns from water to air to woodland,
All wet, full of blooms and smiling.

Genesis

Bound up in homeward thoughts one yellow afternoon,
I saw a lady, aged eleven,
Her dress caught in the broken low branches
Of that miraculous tree, a sudden symbol of her female fear
Too ancient and too high for hands to reach.

Pulled like a parachute above her head,
Holding her on tiptoe,
A white snowmaiden frozen in her dance,
Her shameless white dress showed nipples,
Pale skin, pink underthings with lace and hearts,
Premonitions of female stirrings only half imagined.
Leaning in the wind, her scarlet face turned away from me.
Her eyes brimmed with tears while her useless sister
Screamed in circles around the green mystery,
That tree born before time was, tempting her to climb.
Are you stuck? said I. Bravely she nodded.
May I help? said I. Yes, mister, Her eyes full of grave misgivings.
Undone, she smoothed her dress and looked up.
Undone, she looked beyond me. Perhaps to the eastern edge of Eden.

As I turned to go, the Angel of God appeared at the door.
Surveying the tree and the beloved daughter, this tall apparition
Of heavenly vengeance rushed toward me across the lawn.
Only Eve's thank you, mister killed the murder in his eyes.
Peace, fierce father, I thought.
There will come a time soon enough for real temptations.
Even now, the tree whispers.
Red apples grow from fragile blossoms.

Christmas Poem

In the bleak white wind of this December
I hang lights on the white pine outside the front window.
It is afternoon. The colors are dim against the cold air.
But now, this night, bulbs glow in clusters against green needles.
Inside this bright constellation I see a robin clutching a branch.
His eye is fixed on me. Still as ice.

The bird shines orange and dark in the midst of colored lights
Like an ornament placed just so by children.
Behind another branch, the vaporous ghost of another robin.
And then another. I leave the lights on through the night
Just this once, thinking that Christmas will save the birds.

In this sudden way, robins have touched this season's myth.
They perch now in the shadow of our allusions.
They do not know the story of the child, the manger,
Nor did Christ know our birds among the myriads
Born and dead since that First Birthday.
And yet, seeking heat, puffed with cold and famine,
They move me with their tangency. I am the accidental savior,
While the birds are merely birds in this blind, infinite random.
I think, sometimes, there is only a little meaning in things,
But still the elegant simplicity of bird, tree, and Christmas
Touches some mystery, some meaning that eludes me
Until I remember that the spirit is always mystery,
Never contained in the easy names of things.

Tomorrow the lights will go out. The robins

Will flutter into the shapeless air, recede into distance,

Like ink marks scratched on the cold, paper-thin surface of the sky.

But tonight, bird and Christmas glow into one story,

And the fragile nexus cheers us. A small turning in the dark

That brushes against us like forgotten music suddenly remembered.

Young Galileo

One night while distant phonographs
Wore out the jangling music of the evening,
And males called to females from dormitory windows,
From roofs, from gardens, and from behind hedges,
And the dance of innocence was in full swing
Across a campus littered with the bodies of the living,
And girls and boys in boots ate pizza in the dark
And bearded eighteen year-old prophets
Called for an end to foreign wars,
I stopped to watch a young man on a street corner
With a compass, a tripod and two straws, measuring the speed of stars.

And I said, "good evening, Galileo.
How stands the universe at nine o' clock?"
He smiled thinly, remarking that the chill
Went through his eagle-painted leather jacket,
That the sidewalk was hard under his tennies,
That everyone had gone to the Thunderball Go-Go
For beer, pretzels and romance,
and that Fomalhaut, a star, had moved two degrees in as many hours.
Of that, he couldn't think what more there was to say,
But there it was. Plain as compasses and straws could make it.

Across the street, Guns and Roses sang from giant plastic jukes,
But in the heavens Fomalhaut had moved two degrees.
"The rock and string hanging from this tripod gismo
Make your compass parallel to earth," he said.
"One straw you stick on the North Star. That's your azimuth.
The other's fixed on Fomalhaut. Every two hours

You check your star against your azimuth," he added wearily,
Flicking the plumbline with his leather thumb,
And jaded by the far reaches of his astronomic knowhow.

He pulled his jacket close about his neck,
Sighed, and screwed his face into the nightwind.
"All this to see a star move two degrees," he said,
Lapsing into bitter melancholy.
"For this I miss my foam and chips."
Then he squinted into his straw and gave a start.
"It's moved again," he said.
"Way out there, it keeps on moving."
I knew of course that what he saw
Was the moving earth, not the stars.
But perhaps this young Galileo was seeing with his heart.
A star was drifting across the face of eternity.

"You seem to be getting some action," I said
As we balanced on the rim of the vertiginous earth.
"Yeah," said Galileo. "Three degrees. already. How about that?"

And so it was that he and I sat down together
And spoke of Fomalhaut, ancient music, lost cities,
Voices from the sky, ships of gold and other starry things.

ALL LIFE
MATTERS

Mercy

Sitting in the living room on a blue afternoon,
I express to my sons this lovely, summer sentiment:
The Moles are fucking up my lawn again.
I'm going to set a hundred traps and kill the little bastards.
I had hoped for something offhand, but clever. A gentle irony?
Perhaps a rhyming couplet? Something pastoral?
But no, the moles were not creatures of nature--
They were blind and evil, small devils
Who would eat my children if they could.
At night I dreamed they lived in my intestines,
Nosing into my lungs and liver, drinking my blood.
And so, one summer morning, full of hate,
I set a dozen steel traps in my lawn and garden,
A dozen traps with thick, coiled springs
I could barely stretch to their notches.

For three days the traps crouched ominously, stuck in the earth.
On the first morning I swore they had rearranged themselves,
Small metal monsters from another planet rising out of the soil,
Restless and clever, winking in the sunlight.
Then, one afternoon, I heard the ominous Ka-Chung.
Looking out, I saw that one had sprung.
I pulled it gently from the earth, and there,
Hanging from the trap, a steel spike
Through Its shoulder and another through its stomach,
Something limp and beautiful, trembling, and curled around its pain.

A gray and white creature with small hands.
I saw its fingers open, reach out,
Digging where they found no purchase in the empty air.
It tried again and again to find its way
Into the dark sanctuary where it lived
And did its secret things.

I walked to the wood behind the house,
And with my hands I eased it off its skewer
And let it bleed in the soft soil under a pine sapling.
But its hands would not stop digging,
And I marveled at its patient silence, its quiet industry
As it made its passage into the ground and disappeared.
And then the earth moved for a moment. As if the soil were
    breathing.
Before it died, it knew its home was there, somewhere,
If only hands could find it. And I thought:
God have mercy on small things
That bear their pain and terror in silence,
And God have mercy on those of us who kill them,
Those of us who also reach out in our own blindness,
Hoping to find our place. Digging, digging, here in the dark.

In the Smokey Mountains

In the Smokey Mountains, bees are everywhere,
Invisible in the shadows of trees
And in the tangle of leaves and branches.
One bright afternoon our family of four had lunch by the river.
Red wine, cheese, butter, and then honey
I spread with a spoon on dark bread.
A bit of the golden liquid caught in the creases of my palm,
And more on my fingertips. I could smell it,
As could the bees buzzing over my head.

They landed on my open hand.
Picking their way over its surface,
Their banded abdomens would rise and fall.
Busy in their work, they ignored me.
I was too large to be dangerous.

One found sweetness in the crack between fingernails and flesh.
With slow, patient diligence it cleared the narrow crevice with its pinchers.
Another stood on six legs and moved its black head from side to side.
A third crawled up and down from finger to finger,
Resting only for a moment in the stretch of skin
Between thumb and forefinger
To clean one wing caught in a smudge of honey.
"Happy honeybees!" Cried my son as he snapped a picture.

But were they overjoyed and filled with wonder
On this soft, alien landscape filled with golden surprise?
Or, with their tiny insect brains, were they mindless creatures
Driven only by instinct?

For a moment the world was in my hand.
There was nothing beyond the reach of my fingers
Until suddenly my explorers lifted into the air
And began their homeward journey.

There are infinite universes so vast and unknown
That the stars at night are only an intimation of their being.
There are particles so small they cease to exist
Except as mathematic necessities.
We would all be lost between these unknowable infinities
Were it not for our Faith. Which is that life is sacred.
Rain falls from the dome of heaven and the forest awakens, turns green.
A young woman unbuttons her blouse to feed her newborn.
A buzz of bees gathers honey from my hand.

Birds

So many of them, their feathers stiff, like corrugated paper,
Or soft as air. Eiderdown. All running in lines,
All branching from hollow quill to puff or tuft.
The intricacy of their wings is endless, like their multitudes.
They do not think as we do or remember their generations.
It does not matter when they die.

Once the Dodo waddled on islands in the South Seas.
Once the Giant Moa tried mightily to rule Australia and failed.
Once the Archeopterix perched on Cycad branches,
Its wings like wet flags, gawky and unfoldable.
Once the carrier pigeon looked quick with soft eyes.
But birds are brainless. They do not suffer much.
It does not matter when or how they die.

Birds sing their urge to be in lyric bursts that hurt
Until we remember that to them there is no music.
Their migrations are a great mystery only to us.
Still, they seem to watch the stars during their long journeys
Across Gibraltar, and keep clocks
To know the turning of the stars in different seasons
Across the dark arch of the night.

They follow coastlines and sometimes rivers
And the bright sun that rises one way, sinks another.
But the birds in their multitude of numbers and talents,
In their night songs and wakenings, in their tucks and whirs,
Their one-legged stands, their sudden stillness,
Their swoops and flutters and flashes, plashing into swamps and pools,

Quacking and sputtering and paddling, their quick necks
Turning to look, their eyes like bright buttons,
And their wings, their wings, lift above the earth, rising on
    thermal columns,
They are too much, too many, and their deaths do not matter.

I trace my fingernail through the web of wingfeather in stone,
The gray fossil, its form holding a little, then crushed.
The bones and quills and feathery places all blur and weave
Where some great force busted everything,
And I think: this is the way of things and creatures. To be crushed.
It strikes me to the quick to think there are so many deaths in winter.
The sparrow crushed on the roadside,
The dog with its eyes still open,
The dead cat full of insects.
I tell myself a hundred times it does not matter.

I look now at the bones in my own wrists.
I hold my thin hands up to bright light,
And through the flesh I see, vaguely, my own fossil,
The thing that history will keep.
Something in me frightens, flutters, wants to fly away.
It should be impossible to kill anything

Mouse

If once you have held, in the cup of your hand,
Some small creature. A sparrow, a cricket,
A mouse with bright, pink eyes and twitching whiskers
That looks up at you with a trace of fear
And a trembling uncertain faith in your good will and tenderness,
Hoping for a few crumbs of bread, an ounce of cheese, a gentle touch.
It should be impossible. But still we kill for sport, we kill to eat,
We kill for jealousy, hatred, envy, greed.
We kill to forget our own dark endings.

I once believed in hamburger trees,
(My Aunt Emily told me the buns were grown separately)
But I have sadly come to know
That fish comes from fish, chicken from chicken.
How large and dead the basted and odiferous turkey
Looms on the Christmas table. Again, Aunt Emily to the rescue:
The turkey and Jesus both died
So we could eat, and later go to Paradise.
And to commune with God, I thought, we eat his son on Sunday morning,
And in the afternoon we take the flesh of animals into our mouths.
War, another hunger, means death to thousands.
Even when we lose our appetite for killing, we must go on.
We are men, brothers in battle, faithful to the cause forgotten.

But the mouse in my hand cannot do battle,
Nor is he edible. Not at my table. Still, he must die
Because, according to frightened housewives,
He has the power to squeak and run up their skirts.
When I was seven, I wondered
What he did up there in such forbidden places.

I dream now of the Peaceable Kingdom
Where creatures do not eat each other,
There is no fear of beasts, men have no weapons,
And the mouse sleeps in my hand. Or with the cat.
Winter never comes to make him an orphan,
And all his courage, the tiny spark that keeps him in my hand,
Is brighter, dearer, more urgent
Than knives that cut into meat
Or bayonets flashing in the sun.

Cigarettes for Corporal Mueller

In 296 AD, Menas, a young Egyptian officer, was martyred while serving in the Roman army in Asia Minor because he would not abandon his Christian faith. When his legion brought his remains back to Egypt and buried them, it was noticed that a lamb, and then a princess, were healed of their illnesses when they crossed over his grave. A miraculous spring issued forth from a nearby limestone hillside, a church and then a city were built, and pilgrims came from distant lands to drink and bathe in "the beautiful water of Saint Menas that drives away pain."

South of Tobruk lay the ruins of their defeat:
The English tanks tilted on their haunches,
Or lying on their sides, like wounded beasts
Waiting for the night. And the burning trucks,
The drums of petrol, the twenty-seven men
Gathered in a hopeless circle of blood and hunger.
They watch the black smoke rising in the wasted afternoon.
To the west they see a gray column of the Wehrmact,
Lumbering, breaking the sharp edge of a high dune,
The snouts of their 88 millimeter cannons rising and falling
In the undulating sand. The Panzer Leader
Turns his head. The eagle on his visor flashes.
He shouts an order to his forward column and raises his hand.
Engines idle. Cannons point east across the sand toward Alexandria.

The British smile at the enemy, waiting for death.
The cook pours sand from his helmet. The fusilier stares at the sun.
There is nothing to break the black column of smoke or the circle of
    birds that wheel above them.
No one thinks to raise a weapon,
Not the gray and glittering soldiers of the German Army,
Not the British in their undershirts, soiled with motor grease and blood.

Corporal Mueller squints into the valley of death
And sees a man walking in circles, bleeding from his ears.
Is this the enemy? Is this the British Army? he asks his sergeant.
The sergeant shakes his head. *They have nothing to eat, he answers.*
They have no water.

Water, he thinks. Something vanishes--a silence falls around him,
As if the earth has tilted into another season,
Or a cool silence has flooded the desert,
That stops the sandy wind and changes the light.
The German soldiers stare at one another.
Someone shifts his feet. Another kicks a steel drum
And listens to the hollow sound dying.
Suddenly men spill from the German trucks.
The Panzer troops are everywhere, like elves.
With their quick hands and sharp voices they clean wounds,
Apply pressure bandages. The German Colonel
Orders tins of beef, and salt, and cans of brackish water.
Someone laughs. The wounded fusilier sings *Lily Marlene*.
The English cook, with gestures, sings the line he knows from
    Der Meisterzinger.
When the hot metal begins to burn his fingers,
Corporal Mueller sets his rifle against a burned-out truck.

A British driver, an old man with one arm,
The other buried that morning in a decent Christian ceremony,
Lies in the sand and moves his lips. He asks Saint Menas
To bring him water from the monastery.
His hair is Christmas white, like snow,
His eyes burned out in a month of desert suns.
The German corporal kneels, lifts the old man's head,
And tilts the mouth of his canteen.
You're hurt. Oh God, your wounded, says the one-armed man.
And then he drinks. The shuttle in his throat moves up and down
And he drinks, and drinks again, and gasps for breath.
You're just a boy. Don't worry. I won't let them hurt you.
My God, you're bleeding. Let me get you to the monastery.
The German sergeant, who knows a little English, bends over the
    Corporal's shoulder.
He shakes his head. *He thinks you're wounded. He wants to save you.*
He's a dead man, and he wants to save you!
He wants to bring you to the Holy City!

A half mile away, a British armored unit appears,
The image of guns and turrets shimmering in the mirage of heat.
A sharp command brings Corporal Mueller to his feet.
German soldiers leap into their tanks and half-track trucks.
Hatches down, the Germans rev their engines.

In his field binoculars, the British captain watches.
He sees the circle of the twenty-seven men,
Sees his wounded soldiers drinking water, opening the tins of
    German beef.
Is this the enemy? he asks his sergeant. *Is this the German Army?*
The columns face each other now on opposite hills.
The Panzer Leader and the British captain catch each other
In their glasses and there is a sudden emptiness between them.
The time is neither wrong nor right. An eclipse,
Not of the sun but something else. A shadow, a ghost
That brings time to a standstill. The two commanders
Slowly raise their hands and salute each other.

Seconds before departure, Corporal Mueller leaps from his tank,
For the one-armed man with his crown of white hair is still alive,
Trying now to rise, to wave his hand, to smile.
The Corporal lifts his bones, carries them to the oil fire
Where English soldiers are frying German beef.
We have only small gifts to give, the old man says.
His eyes close as the German soldier holds him close,
Then gently sets him down among his comrades.
The old man's voice turns to water. His eyelids flutter.
He finds the breast pocket of the German uniform,
And for a moment his fingers fumble with the button.

Riding the blind nightmare once again, the Corporal trembles.
He wonders if cities can be built in the desert,
Cities with white buildings rising out of sand
Where strangers come for water and salvation,
And quiet voices fill the cool silence, rising into music.
He knows the story of the desert saint and the miraculous spring
And the Holy City where water flows from the blood of the martyr
To cure the wounded and bring the dead to life.
He shuts his eyes. He is back now in the madness of the sun
As the diesel engines rumble on toward Alexandria.
He forgets now what he will remember later, and forever--
The gift of cigarettes pressed like a bandage against his breast.

The Names

An hour before dawn, the Japanese commanders remind them
That when they strike the American warships,
And metal breaks against metal,
Engines bursting into fire on steel decks, like bright flowers,
The word banzai should be on their lips.
Banzai, as the scream of engines trace the steep descent,
Banzai, a moment before the final shattering of steel and bone
    and blood.

In their quarters, an hour before their flight,
The suicide pilots whisper to each other, saying that instead
They will speak their mothers' names
In that final fiery flight from everything.
One boy, motherless from birth, would say Mishada,
The name of the Geisha he loved passionately, but at a shy distance.
I see them now, the young men who gave their mothers' names to
    those last moments
When thirty-seven ships were sunk at Okinawa.

For days afterwards, invisible beneath the smoky air
Amid the patches of burning oil and the ghosts of dead men,
The names of mothers floated on the water.
Drifting with the wind, undulating, sinking,
Breaking into pieces like sheets of newspaper,
The names of mothers in the water,
There in the great blue, stretching so vast
Between islands that gathered sunlight on beaches for a
    thousand years,
And wheels of circling birds, and flowers without names.

The Gift

Early in the last century they gave us the gift of cherry trees.
Our First Lady and the ambassador's wife planted the first two
At the tidal basin in Washington. Even now, pink blossoms
Crowd the park in Spring, and thousands come to see the colors
Spill and drift over the grass into a sea of love.
After Pearl Harbor, the Bataan death march, and the suicide bombers,
Only the trees remembered what we had forgotten.

We thought it odd that the names of Japanese ships,
Bristling with guns, made us think of flowers, trees, water and sky.
Asahi, the Rising Sun. Fussa, Land of Divine Mulberry Trees.
Akebono, Autumn Clouds. Asagiri, Morning Mist.
We had forgotten war's greatest tragedy: the enemy is born of woman.
He dreams, he loves, and trapped in the sins of emperor and generals
He reaches out, just as we do, for an hour of sky, a day of
    cherry blossoms,
A season of moon and stars.

And at the end when all was lost,
When the silver-gray cloud rose above Hiroshima
Like a white flower blooming,
On that nameless day that vaporized buildings, trees, and children,
Those who gave us cherry trees
And named their ships after clouds and mist,
Once more found words to express the beauty, the mystery, the
    unspeakable horror:
Brighter than a hundred sons, they said.
Brighter than a hundred suns.

LOVE MATTERS

My Mother's Song

I help to make the circle when we meet,
And I have hands that take away your pain.
I cannot wait for praise; I am not quick or fleet.
I am the one who watches you. I am simple, like the rain.

I tell stories full of wonder, and I remember
All the people I have touched in my own time.
I do not conquer men or places; I surrender
To the mystery of roses, melody, and rhyme.

I sense what others feel. I do not think about it much.
The songs I make seem more profound than reason's backward glance.
I share my dreams with anyone. My wisdom's in my touch.
I am not the ballerina others watch. But in my mind, I dance.

The Good Morning

The rusted springs snap against my spine,
And I curse the thin, leaden mattress.
The toilet bowl is brown with iron,
And a slick dampness covers everything.
Sawdust drifts in from my father's junkroom.
At night, something scuttles between the boards.

But my mother, with an enormous, calm sense of what's important,
Fixes eggs in the good morning, pours juice into tin mugs,
Cuts slabs of her own bread. At certain angles
The grain of it shines, like turned earth.

We say our good mornings out on the porch.
The air is thick with summer. Insects buzz
In the field below, the hired man cuts wheat in a vast circle,
Perched like a crow on his ancient tractor, his useless dog running
    everywhere.
Behind the field, the mountain rises in the morning like my
    mother's bread.

My Father in the Mountains

After our long talk on the evils of fundamentalism,
The rape of Sudan and the politics of despair,
All good vacation topics for my father,
We all swam that sunny afternoon
In the high mountain lake.
My sons still children then,
Splashing silver in the bright water,
My mother parting the blue surface with breast strokes,
Her lips pursed against the shallow waves,
My sister swimming easy, face down,
Her long hair undulating behind her shoulders,
My father squatting on a bare rock in his purple shorts,
Thinking of pollution and Southern Baptists.
In gray silence he looks down on us,
Then mumbles that we need to get back.
There are things to do. Appointments (somewhere) to keep.

He sees me coming, underwater.
"It is I," I announce in a low, fishy voice.
"Your friendly neighborhood barracuda."
He gives me a hard, squinty look,
Trying hard not to smile.
"Why is it I am annoyed
To see people having a good time?" he asks.
"That's not normal, is it?"
Once at age nine he prayed to God,
Whose existence he doubted even then.
He prayed he would never, never be normal.
His wish was granted, perhaps, before he asked.

Just another miracle by the hand of the Almighty.
And so my father, who hated religion and swimming,
Entered the water. He splashed in the shallows
Like the child he had never been.

He was the child who had prayed just once
To that large and beautiful improbability
That floated out of reach
Somewhere beyond the mountain lake.

Two Poems with Moons

1

With your tall, awkward grace, your confident elbows
Your smile like a burst of white flowers,
You are all walking and pointing. A surprise
in a floppy hat. A sudden, brilliant burst of...
Something or other. You are eggplant and roses.
Your voice is like air through a field of heather
While your laughter and your easy eloquence
Are like the noise the moon makes in my head.
You are, in short, a wonder that cannot be spoken.
Words, as these lines prove, reach out for you, and miss.
They stumble over your smile. Which is big. Like wind.

2

Sleeping with you, I am innocent again.
The friendly night is painted blue
And the thin, chalky profile of the moon smiles in serene amusement
At the five-pointed silver stars dangling from invisible threads
And tinkling in the solar wind.
It is your love and laughter that keep me young and full of visions.
You turn to me in sleep and make love-moans,
And bid me take off my dream slippers.
There, in the dark, I touch the moon's nose
And walk barefoot in a field of stars.

If You Were Blue

If you were blue
I would never put you in a box
For blue things.
You would be anonymous there.
And lost.

In a dark room
I would never catch you in hard light.
Hard light reveals all the fussy little things,
All the angles and dips and bulges north and south,
And you are not the map of your body.

You are the moment when you happen,
And the moment is not a place, not a stillness.
It exists in the act of coming and going,
And thus, you are nowhere in particular.

But it's true I sometimes find you in what you touch--
The avenues where street sounds gather around you,
The cat that sleeps on your stomach,
Books you read, the scratching of your pen on paper.
A lady once said that when you enter,
The whole room lights up. Well, of course.
You are the room, and you are the entering into the room.
I could have told you. I could have told everyone,
But you, my love (as I have been trying to explain!),
Are in the being, not in the telling.

Cat

Your new cat hides in a soft corner of your crowded closet,
A shapeless pool of golden fur amid the boxes
And soft folds and hangings, where he is anonymous.
Not quite invisible.

At night, safe in the dark, he comes out into your rooms,
Sits in chairs, knocks over bottles in the bathroom,
And noses into cushions and underwear. Each night
He is bolder, eager for the touch of his human mother,
His meow a tender annoyance at three in the morning.

If nothing else were possible,
I would be your cat in the closet.
I would come out at night and guard your sleep,
And be there in the morning with my nose
In your armpit, waking you at six
To sit with you at table for your tea
And spoonful of peanut butter.
I would keep watch all day,
waiting for your return.

We are brothers, the cat and I.
Both faithful, both hopeful, living only in the moment,
Baffled by the dreadful complexities of time,
Steadfast in our love of all we know of you.

Mindy Sunshine

She came in the winter, scratching at the backdoor window,
Starving and close to hopeless, her eyes wide as buttons.
I turned to see a gray kitten behind the glass,
Clawing at the light, at the warmth, at the moving shadows.
She was abandoned, lost, the last of a dead litter,
And if I had known then, I would have thought
That death was a heavy burden for such a small creature,
A heavy thing to carry everywhere she went.

I wondered what my hands and my voice meant to her
Those first few days when she came out of the white December
And into my kitchen, my sofa, my bed.
My two ancient cats, easily annoyed but without claws,
Hissed and batted at her, but to no avail.
To her the house must have been a dream
Of love and play and food and warm places.

During her first illness, and then the second,
I came to know the dark thing that ran in her blood,
But she came back each time, leaping over death and into my arms.

Now, after ten days there is still a smudge on the window,
Fur under the sofa, and a cat smell on the basement stairs.
The night is full of small expectations. I wait
For scratching and mewing at the window
As she climbs the screen and looks in.

A cat's death is a moment's loss, a small sentiment,
A candle in a window that opens
To the vast, impersonal canopy of stars.
A small life slips by, and we move on.

But if I were still a child, I would say
There were paw-prints on my heart.
If I were a child, I would cry at night
And see her ghost in every window.
If I were a child, I would know
That no life is more precious than another,
And that her gratitude, her trust,
Her small, perfect love were good as any.

FAREWELLS
MATTER

Nothing Can Be Enumerated
When All Things are One

Just before dawn the air is heavy with expectation
As the whisper of wind in grass awakens you.
I sleep on, dreaming of the blueberry summer ten years earlier,
Walking with my mother and father in the forest rising into mountains.
On the high porch, you are busy with tea and sunrise.
It has rained during the night, and from the railing
You see white mist roll across the two valleys.
An hour later I find you in my mother's chair.
There is a sweet stillness in the air, and the world is bright and silent.
You have your tea, your book, your morning dress,
and I imagine, still half asleep, that I have promised you a row of beans,
Another of romaine, a circle of golden tiger lilies to bloom next Spring,
And a white fountain that spills silver into the river
Where, tomorrow, I will scatter my parents' ashes.
In this wide place we have nothing to say.
We speak only to hear each other's voices
As if, somehow, the deep earth has said everything.

Tomorrow all our friends will come out of the mountains
To form a circle, a great nexing beyond the makeshift separation
Of here and there, things and other things, the dead and the living.
My mother and father are alive with us,
And in this quietude, we will all be with them, happily deceased.
I will wash my hands in the stream behind the meadow
Where we will all spread our handful of ashes.

The sound of the morning lark is synonymous with the odor of pine,
The rasp of cicadas assent to the morning silence,
And you, my love, you flowing (and flowering) into everything,
You are perfect in your chair on this morning that has never ended.

A Posthumous Poem
for My Mother

WHO THOUGHT ALL POEMS SHOULD RHYME

You were the high clear curve of summer air
That drifted above me everywhere,
And mountains where I made my rhymes,
You made them safe for me to climb.
The forests and the rivers too
Were eloquently parts of you.
So take a poor man's cup, a simple thing,
And take this limping verse, this broken wing.
Like sunlight, you're too large to thank.
You were the cup from which I drank.

Father

There were questions I hoped to ask,
But I thought there was another year, another season
Before the rains would come, the final storm
That would bear you away.
In July I saw how the years had wounded you.
Only your eyes darted, blazed, remembered.
Your eyes followed everything you could not.
So quick, they became your wings
In a world you could not walk.
But you remembered in sudden, stuttering flashes
All the surging and all the boiling over of your youth.
The high sail of your white raven cutting the Connecticut coast.
The barn you built in the woods of New Jersey
For horses that ran up mountains
And across the long meadows of the yellow summer
Where the mysteries of the wood were an odor,
A scent of green, a pulse in the blood.

There were questions I hoped to ask,
But I thought there was another year, another season
Before the rains would come. Why did you love the color blue?
Why did you draw pictures of deer by moonlight when you were forty?
Did you fall in love secretly, when you were fourteen,
And through the years did you remember?
Did you, in your passionate atheism, ever have doubts?
Did you feel a narrow space between midnight and one
When shadows moved in your bedroom?
Did you hear in music the voices of the dead,
And was this the intimation of God, lovely and nearly invisible,
Like a woman standing in a waterfall?

Did you want your ashes scattered in the mountains?
Did you find your place, the thing you so long looked for?
Were you happy in the mountains of Georgia
Where you loved the silver lake and the blueberry summers
And the rising mist at seven in the morning
And the hawks, like hieroglyphs cut against the bowl of blue sky,
Making circles from horizon to horizon?
Did these things speak to you?
Shape the name of something you never spoke?

There were questions I wanted to ask,
But I thought there was another year, another season
Before the rains would come.
But still, I feel your answer in the air.
You are the hawk that rises above the Georgia mountains,
And you are the green wind that comes before sunrise.
You are my father, my own,
The voice that sings inside me.

November

It rains sometimes in the morning.
Sitting at the breakfast table I look out the window.
The earth is warmer than the air,
And this silent collision
Makes fog that turns the trees to ghosts
And erases the woods further in.
The season whispers in my ear.
I try not to listen.

But flowers in the garden
Whose names I have never learned
Still bloom in the freezing air.
In a shelter of petals
The thin stalks that bear the white pollen
Tremble now in the faintest trace of wind.
The flowers and I are grateful for these few days
Of rain and mist that come before ice and snow.

I must not say too much.
Words are like the wind that blows away
The little that still blooms in this weather.
I press my hand against the cold window
And feel the absence that moves inside me.

But know, Dear Lady, that for an hour, or a day,
Memory defeats the threat of the coming winter
And the past lives fiercely and tenderly in the present.

And every morning, in every season,
In the rain or in bright sunlight,
There are always two cups on my table.

The Poet at Eighty-Five

In this late season, the death of the heart is what we fear.
We identify with scarecrows in October fields,
And we are slow in the morning. We sleep too much and too late,
And the rising sun is blood behind our closed eyes,
The color of a migraine, and its shimmering light
Is like the buzz of a dial tone when we reach the telephone too late.

We grow old in clothing stores where nothing fits,
And rows of suits hang anonymous, inert, and headless.
Unable to sleep, we watch black and white dramas at one in the morning.
We see the turns, intonations, and gestures of another age,
And the actors, all dead, are milky ghosts caught forever
In cowboy deserts, in dim cafes, in faded living rooms.

We are sojourners in the vast hallways of Wal Mart and Krogers
Where, in our dotage, we begin to suspect the grand design, the
    final meaning.
We pass bottles in bright colors, their exploding patterns so insistent,
And their moral imperative spelled out in vitamin lists and smiling
    testimonials.
There is a secret meaning in the oatmeal additive in Aveeno,
And we carefully smell the apple essence in green shampoos
And read the ingredients in soup cans. We try to understand
The deep rhythm, the redundancy, the artful insistence
That shows forty pictures of the pretty lady cleaning her toilet,
And the man in the swamp with a crocodile. We take note.
Will the man survive? If so, why? We must come back tomorrow.
We almost catch life's meaning in the syncopations of these,
Our grainy and discontinuous days, and how they coalesce

Into months and seasons, diurnal patterns expanding
Into planetary motions, and then to cosmic stillness.
We are curious and vague, like children
Hearing flute music in an empty cathedral.
We suspect, suddenly, that God is only powerful in his absence,
That we are not meant to know, And that the green lawns
And the wide silence of suburbs
Are the metaphors of our own waiting.

Even so, we are eloquent and sly in ways that youth cannot imagine:
Eloquent in our dreams, floating in the underground river of our desires,
Sly in all we do not understand as we hold forth, amazed by our
    own words.
We are passionate in small things: snags rising above the green forest,
Their sharp, broken limbs angling into the clean air,
More dramatic in death than they ever were in life.
Marbles, cloudy like the eyes of blind men,
Rattling across wooden floors, clicking as they touch
In dusty attics where children play on Sunday afternoons.
And on the boulevard, the smell of gabardine and the flash of long
    summer hair,
And the sound of hushed voices on soft, shadowy afternoons.

We begin again. Gathering in our hands what seems good and wise,
We ride on the wind to reach sun and stars, as we did when we were
    seventeen.

An Old Woman Speaks to Her Husband about the Nature of Things

The sunrise, my love, is filled with small deaths.
Leaves, even in late Spring, blow across lawns,
A voiceless, inarticulate scratching and murmuring.
A mystery, like the shadows of wings plunging into green valleys.
In the North Woods, things come and go. Shattered trunks
And black branches rot on islands in the Boundary Waters
While ferns and finger-shoots of pine
Pierce the stench of death. Here in Edwardsville a rose blooms,
And a jay's head and a broken wing stink in the Spring garden.

As we dream out lives away in this late magic,
I see that nothing lives or dies except in its particulars:
Fifty miles away in the middle of the city
A bullet breaks the fragile arterial housing of the blood.
And here, a gerbil--once trembling in your cupped hand,
Sensing in its small way your enormous human love--
Is stiff now in its cage. In our garden
An earthworm, content in its moist blindness,
Hardens in a dry season.

The stupendous patterns all settle to these trifles,
And in the book where everything is written
There is a place for small animals, and for blades of grass.
The sparrow in the brush is not forgotten.
Nor you, my dearest love. Nor I.

If in This Journey
Toward Shadow

If in this journey toward shadow, I should go suddenly,
My hands turned white, my eyes open in the dust,
If I should stumble to a sudden place, a crevasse,
A falling into unreachable cold caverns,
Why then you must not follow. You must go your way
In what time remains.

I will wait for you as the yellow leaves wait for winter,
As the air, all unknowing, waits for rain,
Or for a change of seasons. I will wait
As dust settles on furniture in deserted houses.

I think sometimes that death is like walking into a closet
Full of empty hangers. The door closes behind,
The light burned out, and no way to turn.
And then again it may be a falling into light
Where I can reach out and touch the edge of some great notion
That precedes all others. In the beginning, they say,
There was a stir of meaning, an instability in the nothing
That bloomed into being.

My dearest one, I will wait for you in whatever place there is or is not.
It was once known that something must always come from nothing,
And that the dead tear apart their shrouds for love.

Sky Music

The Hungarian prodigy engulfs the concert hall
With Beethoven's thunder and lightning,
Then a hush after the storm, a slow drift
Into Lotus Land and moonlight.
But later when the concert hall is silent
I sometimes wonder where the music goes.

Perhaps it seeps like fog into the streets,
Into cafes where men drink beer,
And then moves beyond the ragged silhouette of human life
Into the sky, where there is only silence.
Here all the music of the earth,
All the sounds of our thinking and feeling,
Are lost in the hush of eternity.

Past the improvisations of the moment
Our brave music is soon lost,
And the terrible fear comes once again, unbidden:
Like our music, do we end in silence?

But one night, standing on my roof, I was sure I saw pianos
Drifting in the sky somewhere between Orion and Far Centauri.
Long lines of Bozendorfers floating in the dark spaces between the stars.
Black Steinways in long V's, like flocks of geese against the moon.
Baldwins, like ravens in slow flight
Across the seven-armed Andromedian galaxy.
Pianos with wings, their music infinite and unending,
Soaring toward the great light we have never seen
but always hoped for.

Final Soliloquy of the Man Who Disappears

I am always in the shadows,
Always near the surface where the water
Glints with sunlight and illusion,
And I too am shallow, too easily moved
By the obvious, the too-often told.
I love it when the whistle moans, the engine gathers steam,
And the girl on the platform is left behind,
Her face dissolving into tears.
I love it when the coach begins to move,
And the face of the man in the window turns away.
The music rises in a minor key with violins
As the night train roars out of the midnight station.

Ah, choked with these hearts and flowers
My pool is now too shallow for drowning.
Soon comes a month when water sinks into mud,
And later the wind blows over cakes of cracked earth
And once again I am impatient for a season of rain and desire.
I throw myself against everything impossible
And hope you never read this, never understand
I would be content with you, with you alone,
If we had a place to sleep, a morning sunrise,
Music, dark bread, tomatoes and cheese.
I am a lovely man to know slightly.
And, as I tell the same stories
And sing the same songs over and over,
I grow thin and pale. People see through me.
And then   and then   I disappear

Author's Note

The military poems at the end of section two are based on fact, although I have taken two or three small liberties in dramatizing particular details. To know one's enemy in wartime can mean something very sympathetic and very human.

Acknowledgements

My deepest thanks to the friends who have encouraged and supported Lloyd's writing, including the members of the Alton Writers group. And special thanks to Allison Funk for her very helpful insight into Lloyd's poetry.

- Carolyn Kropp

About the Author

Lloyd Kropp was a member of the faculty at Southern Illinois University at Edwardsville from 1975 to 1992, where he taught poetry and fiction writing, English literature, and an original class in Egyptian language and culture. After retiring as professor emeritus, Kropp continued to write and to travel and give lectures on a variety of interests. He is the author of four widely published novels: *The Drift*, *Who Is Mary Stark?*, *One Hundred Times to China*, and *Greencastle*.

Printed in the USA
CPSIA information can be obtained
at www.ICGtesting.com
LVHW011048030724
784559LV00014B/635